Everyone Travels

J. Jean Robertson

Rourke Educational Media

rourkeeducationalmedia.com

Scan for Related Titles and Teacher Resources

Teaching Focus:

Maps- Locate the color-coded maps in each section. How do the maps help you as you read about different countries? How does the color coding make a difference?

Before Reading:

Building Academic Vocabulary and Background Knowledge

Before reading a book, it is important to set the stage for your child or student by using pre-reading strategies. This will help them develop their vocabulary, increase their reading comprehension, and make connections across the curriculum.

1. *Read the title and look at the cover. Let's make predictions about what this book will be about.*
2. *Take a picture walk by talking about the pictures/photographs in the book. Implant the vocabulary as you take the picture walk. Be sure to talk about the text features such as headings, Table of Contents, glossary, bolded words, captions, charts/ diagrams, or Index.*
3. *Have students read the first page of text with you then have students read the remaining text.*
4. *Strategy Talk – use to assist students while reading.*
   - *Get your mouth ready*
   - *Look at the picture*
   - *Think…does it make sense*
   - *Think…does it look right*
   - *Think…does it sound right*
   - *Chunk it – by looking for a part you know*
5. *Read it again.*
6. *After reading the book complete the activities below.*

Content Area Vocabulary
Use glossary words in a sentence.

aerial
el
gondola
motorized minicars
subways
wheelchairs

After Reading:

Comprehension and Extension Activity

After reading the book, work on the following questions with your child or students in order to check their level of reading comprehension and content mastery.

1. *What is public transportation? What are some examples? (Asking questions)*
2. *How does transportation help people? (Summarize)*
3. *Have you used a taxi before? What kind of taxi was it? (Text to self connection)*
4. *Why do people use many types of transportation when traveling to far places? (Infer)*

Extension Activity

Look through the book and choose a country that you would like to visit. Now think about how you would travel to that country. List all the possible transportation options you have. Which would get you to the country the fastest? Which is the slowest? Which would be the most fun?

What is travel? Travel is how we get from here to there.

India

Children travel to school in different ways. Some walk, some ride bicycles, some go in cars or buses. Some even go by dogsled! How do you go to school?

Africa

North America

Europe

Asia
India

United States

South America

Africa

Australia

United States

SCHOOL BUS

147

When you travel inside a building, you may walk, or ride on an escalator, an elevator, or even a moving sidewalk.

Special **motorized minicars** and **wheelchairs** are made for people who need help traveling. They may be used inside or outside.

Russia

North
America

England

Russia

Europe

Asia

United
States

Africa

South
America

Australia

United States

England

In big cities, many people use public transportation. **Subways**, light rail, buses, cable cars, and the **el** are types of public transportation that many people ride together.

United States

Some people hire taxis to take them places. Some taxis are cars. Some are boats. Others are carts pulled by animals. Some are carts powered by a person riding a bicycle.

North America

United States

South America

Europe

Italy

Africa

Asia

Vietnam

Australia

Italy

Vietnam

North America

Europe

Asia

India

Africa

Mexico

South America

Thailand

Australia

Mexico

Boys and girls who do not live in a city may travel by riding on animals. They may ride a horse, a camel, a burro, or even an elephant.

India

Thailand

France

AIGUILLE DU MIDI

People can travel to the tops of high mountains in a **gondola** or on an **aerial** tramway.

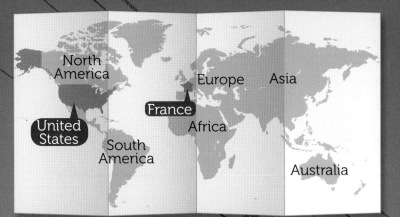

North America

Europe   Asia

France

United States   Africa

South America

Australia

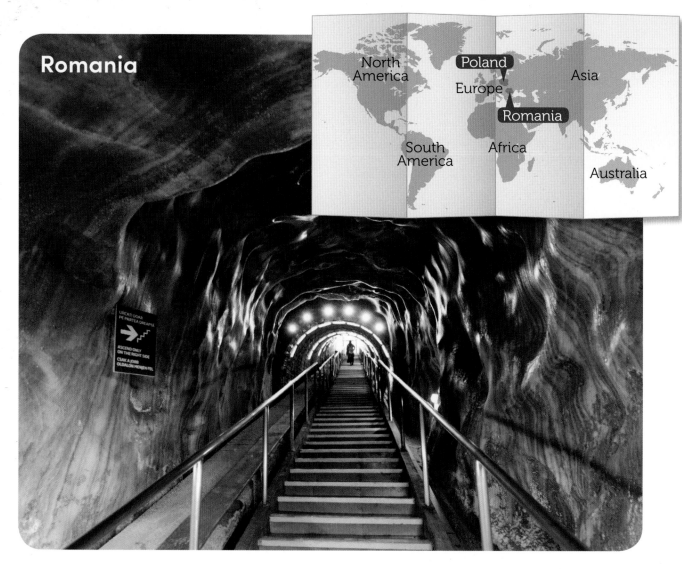

Romania

North America

Poland

Europe

Asia

Romania

South America

Africa

Australia

People can go down into mines on wooden slides or in an underground gondola.

Poland

Some people travel long distances. They may go to other towns, states, or countries. Trains, airplanes, and boats often take people far from home. How many ways do you travel from here to there?

Photo Glossary

 **aerial** (AIR-ee-uhl): Happening in the sky.

 **el** (EL): A city train that usually runs on tracks above the streets.

 **gondola** (GAHN-duh-luh): A cabin or enclosure for passengers.

motorized minicars (MOH-tur-ized MIN-ee-carz): Child-sized cars, with motors, which are fixed so a child with a disability can use them to move from place to place.

subways (SUHB-wayz): Trains that usually run on tracks underground.

wheelchairs (WEEL-chairz): Chairs with wheels. Some are moved by hand and some by motors.

Index

Websites to Visit

www.momsminivan.com/bigkids.html
www.kids-world-travel-guide.com
www.wartgames.com/themes/transportation.html

About the Author

J. Jean Robertson, also known as Bushka to her grandchildren and many other kids, lives in San Antonio, Florida with her husband. She is retired after many years of teaching. She loves to read, write books for children, and travel. She has traveled to a number of interesting countries.

© 2016 Rourke Educational Media

www.rourkeeducationalmedia.com

PHOTO CREDITS: Cover: © Isaak, Jeremy Richards; Title Page: © fishwork; Page 3: © Susan Chiang; Page 4: © Davor Lovincic; Page 5: © Valentin Casarsa, Maciej Bledowski; Page 6: © Monkey Business Images; Page 7: © Carsten Reisinger, dlewiss33; Page 8: © Maria Pavlova; Page 9: © Christoper Futcher; Page 10: © FotograFFF, Davel5957; Page 11: © George Clerk; Page 12: © Cristian Baitg Schreiweis; Page 13: © Oleg Zhukov, Piter Hason; Page 14: © Enrique Silva Del Val; Page 15: © Bartosz Hadyniak, Yuri Arcurs; Page 16: © Kisa Markiza; Page 17: © Raymond C. Roper; Page 18: © PhotoProdra; Page 19: © Eunika Sopatnicka; Page 20: © Maria Pavlova; Page 21: © 06photo

Edited by: Keli Sipperley
Cover and Interior design by: Tara Raymo

Library of Congress PCN Data

Everyone Travels / J. Jean Robertson
(Little World Everyone Everywhere)
ISBN (hard cover)(alk. paper) 978-1-63430-366-8
ISBN (soft cover) 978-1-63430-466-5
ISBN (e-Book) 978-1-63430-563-1
Library of Congress Control Number: 2015931703

Printed in the United States of America, North Mankato, Minnesota

Show What You Know

1. Where would you look to see the el?
2. What are three ways children might travel to school?
3. Name two kinds of vehicles that people often travel in when they go far away.

Meet The Author!
www.meetREMauthors.com

Also Available as:

ROURKE'S
e-Books